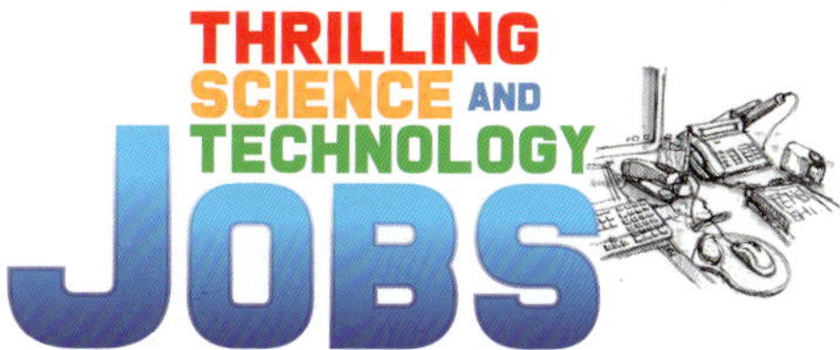

CGI ARTISTS

Ruth Owen and John Willis

AV2
www.av2books.com

Step 1
Go to **www.av2books.com**

Step 2
Enter this unique code

ZCLVKEMR3

Step 3
Explore your interactive eBook!

AV2 is optimized for use on any device

Your interactive eBook comes with...

Contents
Browse a live contents page to easily navigate through resources

Audio
Listen to sections of the book read aloud

Videos
Watch informative video clips

Weblinks
Gain additional information for research

Try This!
Complete activities and hands-on experiments

Key Words
Study vocabulary, and complete a matching word activity

Quizzes
Test your knowledge

Slideshows
View images and captions

... and much, much more!

CGI ARTISTS

Contents

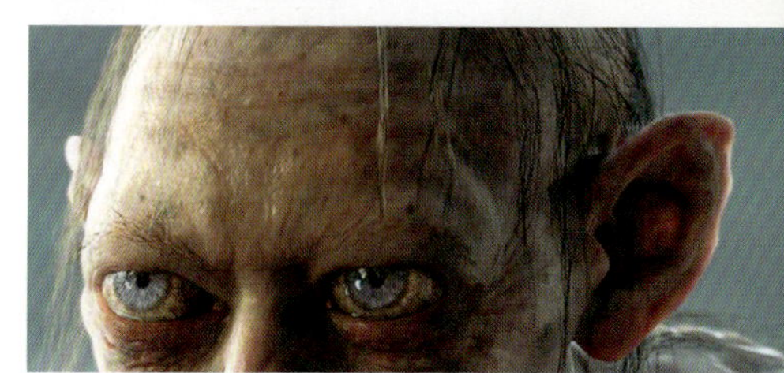

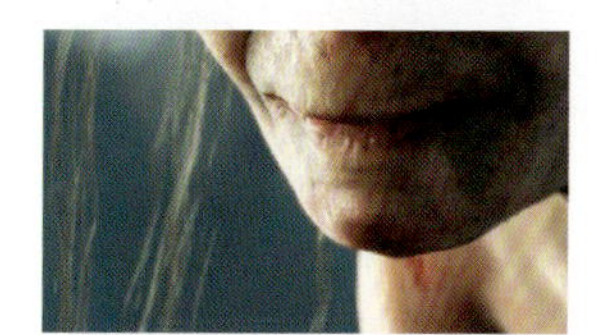

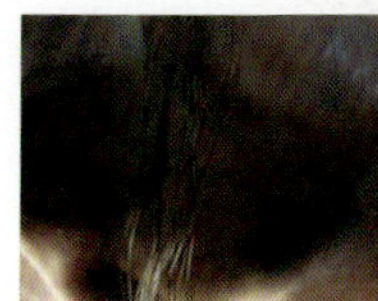

A New Kind of Jungle

In a dark movie theater, the audience falls silent and gets ready to enjoy *The Jungle Book*.

They hold back tears as Mowgli says goodbye to Raksha, his wolf mother. They laugh as the little boy and his bear buddy Baloo get into trouble. Some people cover their eyes in terror as Mowgli battles with the vengeful tiger, Shere Khan. It is hard to believe that the only real thing on the screen is the young actor Neel Sethi.

The movie's jungle setting and the 70 different species of animals that appear are **computer-generated imagery (CGI)**. They only exist because of the skills and creativity of a team of CGI artists!

The millions of hairs on Baloo the bear's body all had to move and catch the light realistically.

Every animal that Neel Sethi's Mowgli interacted with was created through CGI.

MOVIE MAGIC

The Jungle Book is a live-action/CGI film. This means it combines human actors with computer-generated characters and action.

Making Movie Magic

Today, computer-generated imagery can bring to life the ideas of even the most imaginative movie director. But how did **visual effects (VFX)** experts create dramatic effects in the past?

One way was to build miniature models and then bring them to life using a type of **animation** called stop-motion animation. In this technique, a model is photographed. Then, it is moved a tiny amount and photographed again. When the series of photographs, or **frames**, are shown together at high speed, the model appears to be moving.

Stop-motion **animator** Ray Harryhausen produced a famous battle between skeletons and human characters in the 1963 movie *Jason and the Argonauts*. He filmed models of skeletons in stop-motion. Then, he combined the animated fight scene with film of human actors.

In the 1933 movie *King Kong*, the giant ape was actually a model just 18 inches (46 centimeters) high. Its hair was made from rabbit fur.

The **first** stop-motion animation film was released in **1898**. It was called *Humpty Dumpty Circus*.

Ray Harryhausen was known as one of the best visual effects artists. He did the effects for **more than 30** movies, usually by himself.

The skeleton battle in *Jason and the Argonauts* took **four months** to complete for only **four minutes** of footage.

The Nightmare Before Christmas is a 1993 stop-motion animation movie. It had 110,000 frames and took 3 years to film.

Computers Go to the Movies

Audiences were wowed by early visual effects. As computers became a part of everyday life, however, movie makers realized they also offered limitless creative possibilities.

One of the first movies to feature CGI was released in 1982. *Tron* is the story of a computer programmer who finds himself transported inside the **software** of a computer system. The movie's 20 minutes of CGI action were created on a computer that had 500 times less memory than one of today's smartphones.

In 2010, a sequel to *Tron* was made. *Tron*: *Legacy* featured updated CGI effects. The film was nominated for several special effect-related awards.

In 1993, director Steven Spielberg brought dinosaurs back from extinction in *Jurassic Park*. The movie combined life-size **animatronic** dinosaur models, dinosaur suits, and CGI dinosaurs.

Tron: Legacy used CGI effects to make actor Jeff Bridges appear as young as he did in the first movie.

Six minutes of sequences created with CGI were used in *Jurassic Park*.

MOVIE MAGIC

Visual effects expert John Rosengrant played one of *Jurassic Park*'s terrifying, flesh-hungry velociraptors. Wearing a foam rubber suit, he stalked and attacked the movie's human characters. In order to move like a dinosaur, Rosengrant studied lizards and large birds.

Out of This World

In 1995, director James Cameron began writing a movie that was set on an alien moon named Pandora. Cameron knew exactly what he wanted to create, but the technology to do it had not yet been invented. By 2005, advancements in CGI made it possible for Cameron's vision to come alive. That vision was the **groundbreaking** movie *Avatar*.

Cameron brought together a team of the world's best CGI artists. The artists had the chance to create an entire world of huge mountains, giant trees, and fantastical creatures. When audiences watched *Avatar*, they found it hard to believe that every part of Pandora had been created inside a computer!

In May of 2017, Walt Disney World opened the World of Pandora. It is an exact replica of the movie world. Its ride, Flight of Passage, uses visual effects to make the riders feel like they are flying.

Avatar's CGI team developed an entire world of new beings, including six-legged, horse-like creatures, giant, flying dragons, and the Na'vi race that inhabits Pandora.

It could take 47 hours to render a single frame of *Avatar*.

MOVIE MAGIC

The *Avatar* team developed a system called a virtual camera. The actors were filmed running or fighting inside the **studio**. When this action was viewed through the virtual camera, however, the team could see the actors' CGI characters running and fighting inside the CGI world of Pandora.

Where It All Begins

So how do CGI artists bring to life the worlds and characters we love to see on the screen?

The CGI parts of a movie are created by artists who work for a VFX company. A team of artists includes concept artists, **modelers**, **riggers**, texture artists, and animators. It is possible to work in all these areas or to specialize in just one.

Concept artists are the first artists to work on a project. They might make hundreds of drawings or pieces of digital art to develop the movie's characters and scenery. Their work helps the rest of the team understand how the movie's world and characters will look. Once filming starts, they may need to redraw characters and places as the original ideas for the movie change.

The story for a movie is sometimes taken from a book. A concept artist carefully analyzes the author's descriptions of characters, places, and events to bring the book to life. To create their ideas, concept artists might research animals or real-life places such as jungles, mountains, and historic buildings.

Concept artists work with pencils, paint, and computer programs such as Photoshop or Painter.

Where CGI Artists Work

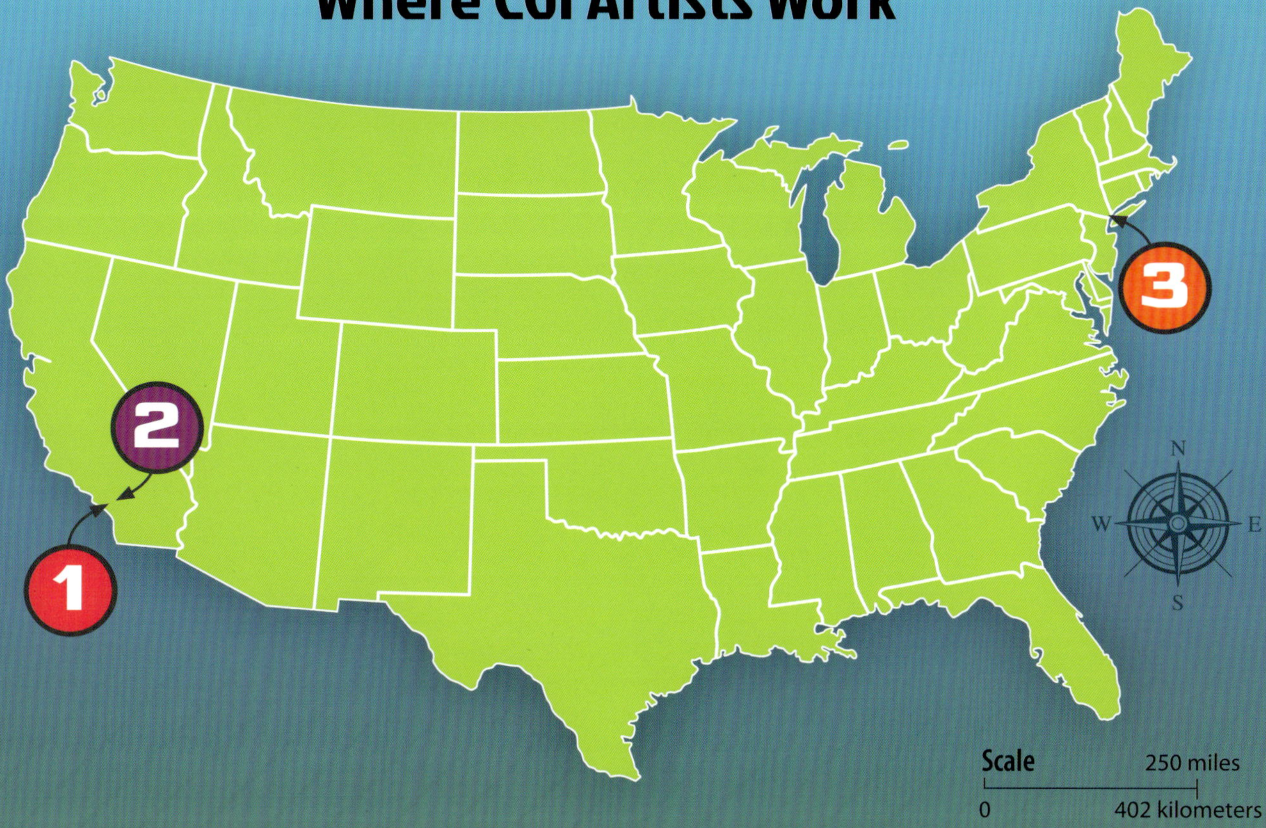

1
2
3
N
W
E
S
Scale
250 miles
0
402 kilometers

Walt Disney Animation Studios, Burbank, California

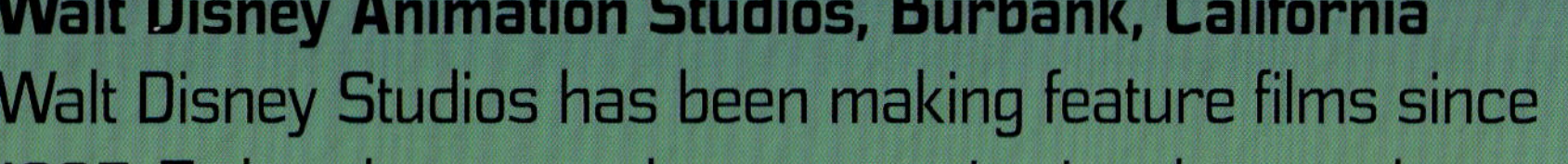

Walt Disney Studios has been making feature films since 1937. Today, they are a large organization that employs many CGI artists. It includes Pixar Studios, 20th Century Fox, Marvel Animation Studios, and Lucasfilm Animation Studios.

Warner Brothers Entertainment, Burbank, California

Warner Brothers Entertainment does CGI work for movies, television, and video games. They have worked on *Harry Potter, The Lego Movie, The Lord of the Rings, Arrow,* and various video games.

The Studio, New York City, New York

The Studio is a female-run CGI studio founded in 1988. They work in mediums including live action, animation, design, and events. They have worked on films and documentaries such as *The Remix: Hip Hop x Fashion*, and been featured in the Midnight Moment in Times Square.

Making Models

The CGI work on a movie goes through a series of stages known as the pipeline. Once the concept artist's ideas are approved, the next stage in the pipeline is modeling.

An artist called a modeler takes the concept artist's ideas and creates a rough **three-dimensional (3D)** model on a computer, using modeling software. Next, using shapes called polygons, the artist creates a more detailed model on the computer.

The modeler might create people, animals, vehicles, a mountain, or a city street. In *The Day After Tomorrow*, New York City is flooded by a tsunami and then frozen under a thick layer of ice. The VFX team used 50,000 detailed photos of New York to create a realistic 3D digital model of the city.

One type of 3D model is called a polygon mesh model. Polygon mesh is the geometric shapes that make up an object.

New York is one of the best-known cities on Earth. The CGI artists knew they had to make their digital New York look 100 percent realistic while working on *The Day After Tomorrow*.

MOVIE MAGIC

When a modeler is creating a model on a computer, he or she might use lots of reference photos to continually check details, such as the length of an animal's tail or the shape of its muscles under its skin.

The Texture Artists

When the modelers' work is completed, the texture artists take over. From fur to wrinkled skin, or brickwork to rusting metal, these artists add color and textures to the computer models of characters, buildings, and landscapes.

Texture artists use software programs to place photos of real-life textures onto models. Sometimes the texture they need, such as the Na'vis' blue skin in *Avatar*, does not exist in real life. In that case, the texture artist must create something new and unique.

The artists who worked on the CGI characters for the *Transformers* movies wanted the robots to look as if they really had transformed from vehicles. To achieve this effect, the artists gathered 6,000 photos of car and truck parts and used them as textures on the models.

The shapes and textures of the floating mountains in *Avatar* were inspired by real-life mountains in China's Zhangjiajie National Forest Park.

In **2010**, for the movie *Tangled*, Disney Animation Studios had to create a **new rendering program** to animate Rapunzel's hair.

London based CGI company **Framestore** created the magical world in the **eight *Harry Potter*** movies and their spinoffs.

In **1992**, a program called **Viewpaint** was used to create a 3D texture map of dinosaurs in ***Jurassic Park***. It was the first of its kind.

Bringing the Models to Life

Once a model—one of a character, for example—is complete, the next steps in the pipeline are to rig it and animate it in the computer.

Animating a model means making it move. The job of a rigging artist is to give a model a digital skeleton. Each of the skeleton's joints is called a "handle" or control point. An animator clicks on the handles to make a model bend and move.

Animation is a very technical job. To make realistic animations, however, an artist must also be creative and pay lots of attention to detail.

Using special software, animators can make a tiger pounce, a warrior fight, or even a torrent of water rush down a city street. Just a few seconds of on-screen action can take hours, or even days, of painstaking detailed work.

Animating a person or animal often requires the animator to start by watching videos of that person or animal moving.

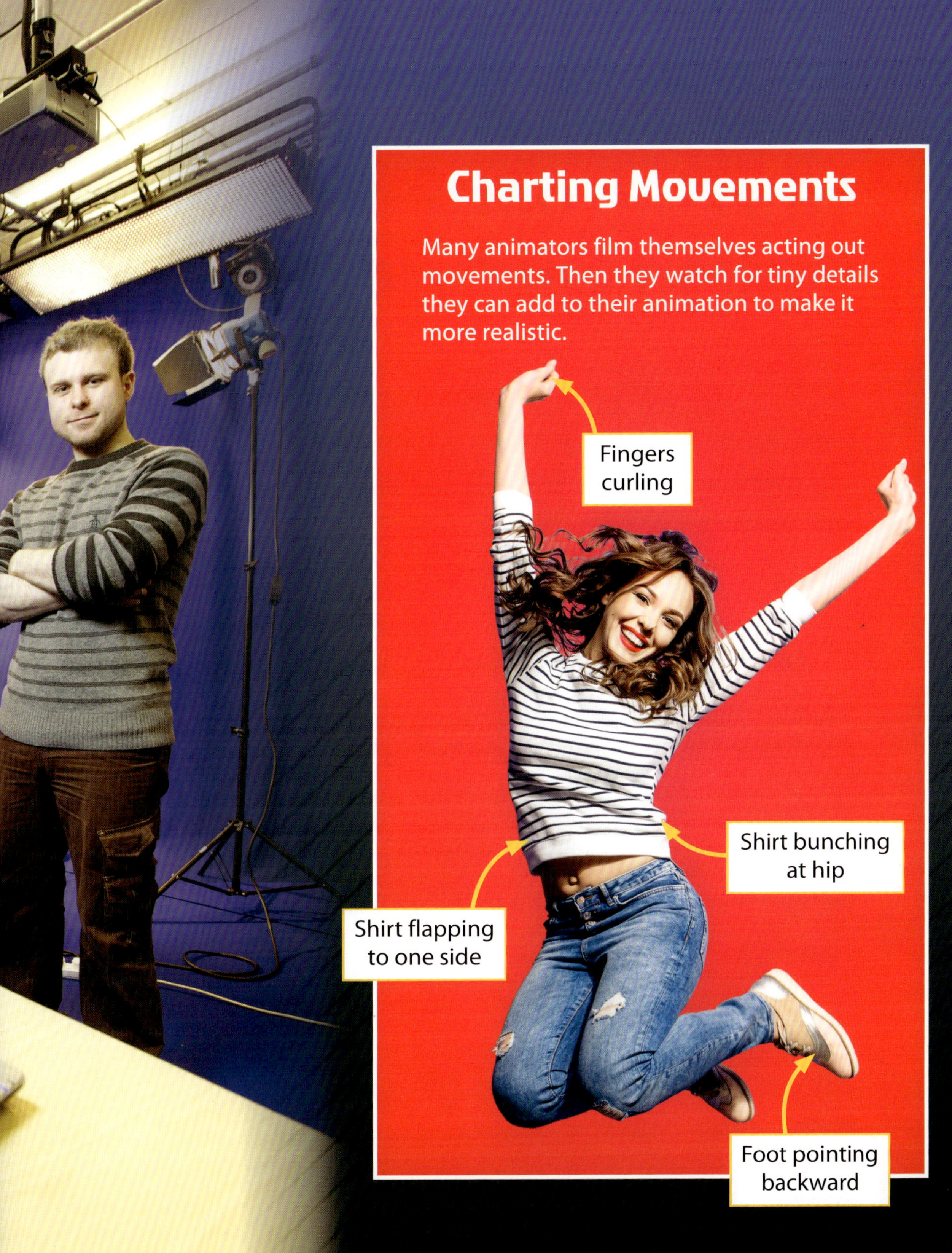

Charting Movements

Many animators film themselves acting out movements. Then they watch for tiny details they can add to their animation to make it more realistic.

Working with Motion Capture

Many animators make their characters move by using only animation software and their own skills. Another way to animate 3D characters is to use **motion capture**, which is sometimes called performance capture.

To animate with motion capture, an actor wears a suit that has markers on it. Cameras all around the set pick up signals from the markers. Then, on a computer, the signals are used to create a moving skeleton of the actor that can drive, or move, the digital character.

Sometimes, facial motion capture is also used. Actors have tracking dots stuck to their faces. A high-speed camera on a helmet mount picks up signals from the dots and captures the actor's facial expressions in great detail. Then these expressions are applied to the CGI character's face.

Video games also use this technology. A Sega video game, *Virtua Fighter 2*, began this trend in 1994. By 1995, this became the most common way to create video games that involved athletes, fighting, or other character-based actions.

Motion capture technology allows for more realistic digital characters than CGI alone.

Andy Serkis is one of the best known motion capture actors. He has played characters in *The Lord of the Rings, Dawn of the Planet of the Apes*, and several *Star Wars* movies.

MOVIE MAGIC

To film motion capture, actors usually perform in a studio, often away from the main action. In *Dawn of the Planet of the Apes*, the filming of the motion-capture work was combined with the main live action—even outdoors.

Creating Gollum

Before there was CGI, movie makers might have put an actor in make-up and a bodysuit to produce a fantasy, human-like creature.

Today, characters such as Gollum, from the *Lord of the Rings* and *Hobbit* movies, are brought to life by CGI artists. Creating and animating humanoid characters and making them look real is not a simple task.

The CGI Gollum has been appearing in movies since 2001. Over the years, Gollum has become more and more realistic. To achieve this, CGI artists researched how skin and eyes react to light. They studied how real skin might slide over his scrawny muscles and bones. To create the effects they wanted, they had to develop new types of software.

Today, when we watch Gollum on the screen, our heads tell us he is not real. Our eyes, however, find that very hard to believe!

All three installments in *The Lord of the Rings* trilogy won the Academy Award for Best Visual Effects.

MOVIE MAGIC

Advances in technology have enabled helmet-mounted cameras to capture increased detail in an actor's performance. Then, performance-capture software applies the actor's emotions to a CGI character.

Back to the Jungle

Every second of *The Jungle Book* takes place in a jungle in India. However, the movie was filmed in a studio in Los Angeles...and then the CGI artists got to work!

The movie's artists gathered more than 100,000 photos of Indian jungles. They used this reference material to create vines, bark, moss on rocks—every detail.

Using CGI to produce a real-life environment was harder than creating a fantasy land like *Avatar*'s Pandora. Details such as sunlight filtering through trees or a character's shadow have to be realistic. We may not think about it much, but our brains know what the real world looks like. If the jungle looked fake, it would spoil the audience's enjoyment of the movie.

The CGI team learned through the process of creating *The Jungle Book* that rocks were actually harder to animate than the rest of the jungle.

MOVIE MAGIC

Some of the movie's animals were larger than real life compared to Mowgli. Director Jon Favreau wanted to create the feeling of what it is like to be a child in a big world.

The Bear Facts

As *The Jungle Book*'s CGI team worked on creating the movie's world, actor Neel Sethi was hard at work in a bare studio. Sometimes, he might have a log or rock to sit on. When he talked to his animal friends, he was often speaking to a crew member holding a puppet.

A scene where Mowgli floats along a river was filmed in a large tank of water—in a parking lot outside the studio. Director Jon Favreau climbed into the water so that Neel had someone to sing to and chat with. Thanks to the movie's artists, what the audience sees in the final movie is a little boy splashing and floating in a jungle river with a large, friendly brown bear.

To understand how a bear might look floating in water, CGI artists studied polar bears swimming in the ocean.

Baloo is so large and furry that each frame involving him took five hours to render.

MOVIE MAGIC

It took a team of around 800 CGI artists to create *The Jungle Book*. From modelers and texture artists to riggers and animators, the team's thousands of hours of work made possible 105 minutes of magic.

Tomorrow's Movie Magic

Using technology, CGI artists can create realistic-looking wild animals and transport audiences to alien worlds. The men and women who work in CGI are not just imaginative and creative. They are also technical wizards who use their skills to discover and invent new ways to use computer power.

In 2019, Disney Animation Studios released a new, photorealistic version of the *The Lion King*. Because all the characters are wild animals, they were created with great care by CGI artists. Later in 2019, it was announced that James Dean, an actor who died in 1955, would be brought back to life on screen in CGI form. A movie, *Finding Jack*, wants to use his likeness as their main actor. This brings moral and ethical questions for CGI artists.

Even today it is sometimes difficult to know what is real and what is CGI. How will it be 10 years from now? What technology will be available to CGI artists 20 years from now? If you are creative and love movies and computers, perhaps you could be one of tomorrow's top CGI artists.

What technology might you help invent? What will your audiences be watching? It is impossible to say. In fact, when it comes to CGI, there's probably only one certainty...

...nothing is impossible!

History of CGI Animation

CGI animation began with the discovery of stop-motion animation more than 100 years ago. From there, many advancements have improved this technology.

1960 The Royal Institute of Technology in Sweden created a 49-second animation of a car traveling down a highway. This was the first of its kind.

1973–1976 *Westworld* becomes the first feature film to show 2D CGI animation. Its sequel, *Futureworld,* becomes the first to show 3D CGI animation.

1995 The first feature-length CGI animation, *Toy Story*, is released. It was added to The United States National Film Registry in 2005 for being the first of its kind.

2004 *The Polar Express* is the first 3D computer-animated film to be created using motion capture.

2009 James Cameron creates an entire CGI world with *Avatar*. It remains the world's highest grossing film for 10 years.

2013 In the movie *Furious Seven*, CGI animators digitally add the actor Paul Walker into the film after his tragic death.

2013 Animators of Disney's *Frozen* create a program called the Matterhorn to animate snow properly.

2019 A new adaption of *The Lion King* is made using new, incredibly realistic CGI technology.

CGI Artist Quiz

01 Who is part of the team of artists at a VFX studio?

02 What system did the *Avatar* team develop?

03 In which film did Ray Harryhausen animate skeletons fighting humans?

04 What animation technique involves an actor in a special suit with dots that track his or her movement?

05 What does a rigging artist do?

06 How many photos of New York did the VFX team look at to create the wave scene in *The Day After Tomorrow*?

07 Where are Walt Disney Animation Studios and Warner Brothers Entertainment located?

08 What program created a digital texture map of dinosaurs in *Jurassic Park*?

09 What does a texture artist do?

10 What is the benefit of helmet mounted cameras in motion capture?

ANSWER

01 Concept artists, modelers, riggers, texture artists, and animators **02** Virtual camera **03** *Jason and the Argonauts* **04** Motion capture **05** Gives a model a digital skeleton **06** 50,000 **07** Burbank, California **08** Viewpoint **09** Adds the proper texture to CGI animation **10** Increased detail in performance and emotion

Key Words

animation: a way of making drawings or computer-generated images appear to move

animator: a person who makes drawings or computer-generated images move. In CGI, animators use computer software to animate images.

animatronic: making a lifelike puppet or model move with electronics or pulleys and levers

computer-generated imagery (CGI): images that are created on a computer with different types of software

frames: still images that, when combined, create a piece of moving film

groundbreaking: being the first to do something; innovative

modelers: computer artists who use modeling software to create 3D digital models, such as animals, vehicles, and landscapes

motion capture: an animation technique in which actors wear special suits that allow their movements to be captured and applied to a CGI character

riggers: computer artists who use rigging software to create skeletons for digital models that will allow an animator to make the model move

software: the programs that are used to operate computers

studio: a large building where movies and TV shows are filmed

three-dimensional (3D): having or appearing to have height, width, and depth, rather than just something flat or two-dimensional

visual effects (VFX): visual tricks that are used in movies and TV shows. Visual effects are created after all the normal filming is done, using miniature models or CGI.

Index

Get the best of both worlds.

AV2 bridges the gap between print and digital.

The expandable resources toolbar enables quick access to content including **videos**, **audio**, **activities**, **weblinks**, **slideshows**, **quizzes**, and **key words**.

Animated videos make static images come alive.

Resource icons on each page help readers to further **explore key concepts**.

Published by AV2
350 5th Avenue, 59th Floor
New York, NY 10118
Website: www.av2books.com

Library of Congress Control Number: 2019957552

ISBN 978-1-7911-2183-9 (hardcover)
ISBN 978-1-7911-2184-6 (softcover)
ISBN 978-1-7911-2185-3 (multi-user eBook)
ISBN 978-1-7911-2186-0 (single-user eBook)

Printed in Guangzhou, China
1 2 3 4 5 6 7 8 9 0 24 23 22 21 20

032020
101319

Project Coordinator: John Willis
Designer: Terry Paulhus

Every reasonable effort has been made to trace ownership and to obtain permission to reprint copyright material. The publishers would be pleased to have any errors or omissions brought to their attention so that they may be corrected in subsequent printings.

AV2 acknowledges Alamy, Dreamstime, iStock, and Shutterstock as its primary image suppliers for this title.

First published in 2017 by Ruby Tuesday Books Ltd.